M000206024

CHOSEN WORDS

FAVORITE
SAYINGS
OF
FAMOUS PEOPLE

Compiled by
Joseph L. Neely

Published in the United States by
Great Quotations Publishing Company
1967 Quincy Court
Glendale Heights, IL 60139

Printed in Hong Kong

To my father, Ralph Neely,
who would have been proud.
To my mother, Catherine Bird,
who surely is.
To Sam, Maren, and Tom;
and especially
with love for my wife, Aleyn.

Special thanks to
reference librarians everywhere.

Dear Reader,

In the fall of 1992 I began writing to successful men and women, asking them to provide me with a saying which had given them comfort, kept them focused on their goals, or inspired them throughout their lives. This book is the result of those letters.

I will always be grateful to the men and women featured in this book, who took a risk by responding to a request from a complete stranger. I hope the sayings they provided will give you some insight into the philosophies and attitudes which help certain people to accomplish significant tasks.

Sincerely,

Joe Neely

Harvey Mackay *is the author of several bestselling books, including* <u>Swim With The Sharks Without Being Eaten Alive</u>. *Mackay is also the founder of Mackay Envelope Corporation in Minneapolis.*

"Find something you love to do and you'll never have to work another day of your life."

Denton A. Cooley, M.D. is a pioneer in cardiac surgery. In 1969, Cooley implanted the first artificial heart in the United States. He was awarded the Presidential Medal of Freedom in 1984. Dr. Cooley is Surgeon-in-Chief at the Texas Heart Institute. He calls the first of the sayings he submitted his personal time saver.

"If a thing is not worth doing,
it's not worth doing well
or at all!"

Do what thy manhood bids thee do,
from none but self expect applause.
He noblest lives and noblest dies,
who makes and keeps self-made laws.

-Sir Richard Burton
(1821-1890), explorer

*Brooklyn's St. Paul Community Baptist Church and its pastor, **The Rev. Johnny Ray Youngblood,** were featured in the book <u>Upon This Rock: The Miracles of a Black Church</u>.*

And we know that all things
work together for good
to them that love God,
to them who are called
according to his purpose.

*-The Holy Bible
King James version*

*Historian **Arthur M. Schlesinger, Jr.**'s has won Pulitzer Prizes for his books <u>The Age of Jackson</u> in 1946 and <u>A Thousand Days: John F. Kennedy in the White House</u> in 1966. Schlesinger served as a special assistant to Presidents Kennedy and Johnson. Schlesinger teaches at The City University of New York.*

Man's capacity for justice makes democracy possible, but man's inclination to injustice makes democracy necessary.

-Reinhold Niebuhr, from his book The Children of Light And The Children of Darkness

Frank Borman was an astronaut in both the Gemini and Apollo space programs. Borman commanded the Apollo 8 flight which circled the moon on Christmas Eve and Christmas Day of 1968.

"Stay in there and pitch."

James S. Brady was President Ronald Reagan's press secretary. Brady was wounded by John Hinckley during an attempt to assassinate Reagan in 1981. Since that time, Brady has worked to limit the availability of handguns in the United States.

Be nice on the way up! Because you never know whom you may meet on the way down.

-unknown

Helen Gurley Brown is the editor of *Cosmopolitan Magazine* and a bestselling author.

"My favorite saying is, *There is no free lunch.* I amend that for my Cosmo readers to say there are plenty free lunches and other terrific rewards if you work your tail off - guts and discipline will get you everywhere."

Benjamin S. Carson, M.D. *grew up poor on the streets of Detroit. Carson rose above the difficult circumstances of his youth and went on to graduate from Yale University and the University of Michigan Medical School. Dr. Carson is the Director of Pediatric Neurosurgery at The Johns Hopkins Hospital in Baltimore, Maryland.*

"Knowledge is the key that makes you into a more valuable person.
And knowledge is best acquired through reading - NOT TELEVISION!"

Martin Buser competed in 8 Iditarod dog-sled races before finally finishing first in 1992. While finishing first, Buser smashed the northern course record by almost 7 hours. He won again in 1994, setting a new course record.

"Run your own race, not your competition's."

Ray Charles *mother gave him two mottos to live by when he was young.*

You may be blind,
but you're not stupid.

In the course of life there are
at least two ways to do
anything. If you can't do
something one way,
do it the other way.

-Aretha Robinson

Marva Collins *is an educator.*
She is the Founder of Westside Preparatory
School in Chicago.

I would rather die
on my feet
than to beg
on my knees.

-a similar saying is attributed to
Mexican revolutionary
Emiliano Zapata

*Illusionist **David Copperfield** has vanished the Statue of Liberty, levitated across the Grand Canyon, walked through the Great Wall of China and escaped from Alcatraz.*

"Whenever I pursued my dreams, I discovered something astonishing - I discovered myself. My secret has been to consider nothing impossible - then to treat possibilities as probabilities."

James C. Dobson, Ph.D., *is the President of Focus on the Family.*

I have concluded that the accumulation of wealth, even if I could achieve it, is an insufficient reason for living. When I reach the end of my days, a moment or two from now, I must look backward on something more meaningful that the pursuit of houses and land and machines and stocks and bonds. Nor is fame of any lasting benefit. I will consider my earthly existence to have been wasted unless I can recall a loving family, a consistent investment in the lives of people, and an earnest attempt to serve the God who made me. Nothing else makes sense.

-from Dr. Dobson's book
What Wives Wish Their Husbands Knew About Women

Charles W. Colson is the founder of the Prison Fellowship Ministries. Colson pleaded guilty to charges related to Watergate and served seven months in prison. In 1993 he was awarded the Templeton Prize for Progress in Religion. Previous winners of this award included the Rev. Billy Graham and Mother Teresa.

I have learned to be content whatever the circumstances. I know what it is to be in need, and I know what it is to have plenty. I have learned the secret of being content in any and every situation, whether well-fed or hungry, whether living in plenty or in want. I can do everything through Christ who gives me strength.

-Philippians 4:11-13

Erma Bombeck's favorite saying comes from the musical 'Pippin'. She described the character who speaks these lines, Charlemagne's son, as being 'restless, full of life and ready to take risks.'

Can't you see, I want my life to be something more - than just long.

-from the musical Pippin, book by Roger O. Hirson, music & lyrics, Stephen Schwartz

*Race car driver **Stan Fox** has finished among the top ten racers three times in the Indianapolis 500.*

"Life is like a ride on a pendulum -
enjoy it while you're on
the top."

William Friday *is President Emeritus of the University of North Carolina.*

But be ye doers of the Word, and not hearers only, deceiving your own selves.

-James 1:22

Arnold Palmer *has won more than 90
major golf tournaments, including four
Masters Championships.*

If you think you are beaten,
you are;
If you think that you dare not,
you don't;
If you'd like to win,
but think you can't,
It's almost certain you won't.
If you think you'll lose,
you've lost;

For out in the world you'll find
Success begins with a fellow's will-
It's all in the state of mind.
If you think you are outclassed,
you are;
You've got to think high to rise;
You've got to be sure of yourself
before
You can ever win a prize.
Life's battles don't always go
To the stronger or faster man;
But soon or late the man who
wins
Is the man who thinks he can.

-unknown

Col. David H. Hackworth (ret.) is America's most decorated living military veteran. The recipient of 8 purple hearts and more than 100 valor awards, Hackworth considers his highest honor to be the United Nations Medal for Peace he was awarded for anti-nuclear work.

"War is easy to get into and hard to get out of."

Larry Hagman is an actor who has starred in several long-running television series.

"Don't worry,
be happy,
feel good."

*The **Rev. Theodore M. Hesburgh, C.S.C.** is President Emeritus of the University of Notre Dame. He is also a respected educator and author.*

One of the greatest modern heresies that I hear from time to time is that in our modern world one person cannot make a difference. I do not believe that for one moment. I know it is factually inaccurate. And I never hesitate to say so, especially to our students at Notre Dame. One person or group of persons can make an enormous difference in our lives and our way of living. Dr. Albert Schweitzer did, Rachel

Carson did, Mother Teresa did, Tom Dooley did, and Jim Grant did. History is replete with heroic people who realized that they could make a difference, and did despite the conventional wisdom of the day.

-from his book, God, Country, Notre Dame
Doubleday Publishing, Inc.

Lou Holtz *is the head football coach at the University of Notre Dame*

Trust in the Lord
with all your heart.
On your own intelligence,
rely not.

-Proverbs 3:3

Alexander M. Haig, Jr. has served as White House Chief of Staff, Supreme Commander of N.A.T.O. and Secretary of State. He is currently the President of Worldwide Associates, Inc.

"Patriotism has always been an expression of the willingness of an individual to dedicate a certain portion of himself, his talents and energies, to something beyond himself. To adopt for himself the basic values that have made our nation what it is, and to be willing to struggle - and if necessary to fight - for those values."

*Legendary blues musician **John Lee Hooker** has two favorite sayings.*

"Nothin' but the best
and later
for the rest."

"Take your garbage
to the city dump
'cause I can't use it here."

Gordie Howe *is the greatest hockey player of all time.*

"Give yourself a choice and not a chance. Give 100% to your school work and 100% to your sport...then when the time comes, you are able to make your choice about what you wish to do in life."

Dr. Diane M. Komp, M.D. *is a Professor of Pediatrics at Yale University's medical school. She has written two books on children with cancer. Her most recent book is A Child Shall Lead Them.*

I love these little people; and it is not a slight thing when they, who are so fresh from God, love us.

-from Charles Dicken's Old Curiosity Shop

Rabbi Harold Kushner is the author of many books, including <u>When Bad Things Happen to Good People</u>.

Those who trust in the Lord will have their strength renewed.

-Isaiah 40:31

*In addition to gaining fame as an actor and comedian, **Jerry Lewis** is a tireless fund-raiser in the battle against muscular dystrophy.*

I shall pass through this world but once. Any good, therefore, that I can do or any kindness that I can show to any human being; let me do it now. Let me not defer nor neglect it, for I shall not pass this way again.

-unknown

*A star on television for many years, **Art Linkletter** is also an author and popular speaker. Linkletter's favorite saying comes from another contributor to this book.*

Things turn out best for the people who make the best of the way things turn out.

-John Wooden

*The late **Thomas P. 'Tip' O'Neill, Jr.*** *served as Speaker of the United States House of Representatives from 1977-1986. Thomas P. O'Neill III read this poem at his father's funeral. This poem was originally given to Speaker O'Neill by James Michael Curley, Boston's colorful 4-term mayor.*

<u>Around The Corner</u>

Around the corner I have a friend,
In this great city that has no end;
Yet days go by, and weeks rush on,
And before I know it a year is gone,
And I never see my old friend's face,
For Life is a swift and terrible race.
He knows I like him just as well
As in the days when I rang his bell
And he rang mine.

We were younger then,
And now we are busy, tired men:
Tired with playing a foolish game,
Tired with trying to make a name.
"Tomorrow," I say, " I will call on Jim,
Just to show that I'm thinking of him."
But tomorrow comes -
and tomorrow goes,
And the distance between us
grows and grows.

Around the corner! - yet miles away ...
"Here's a telegram, sir ..."
        "Jim died today."
And that's what we get,
and deserve in the end:
Around the corner, a vanished friend.

-Charles Hanson Towne

*Religious leader **Ruth Stafford Peale** is the Chairman of the Board of the Peale Center for Christian Living. Like her late husband, the Rev. Norman Vincent Peale, she is a popular author and speaker. The Peales founded Guidepost Magazine.*

"There are three answers to prayer; yes, no, and wait awhile. It must be recognized that no is an answer."

*Major league umpire **Steve Palermo** was wounded while chasing an armed robber. Palermo is learning to walk again, and hopes to return to major league baseball. He submitted 2 favorite sayings.*

Inch by inch, life's a cinch.
Yard by yard, life is hard.

-unknown

Difficult things take a long time.
The impossible takes a little longer.

-unknown

Gloria Steinem *is a feminist, political activist, and bestselling author.*

If our dreams weren't already real within us, we could not even dream them.

-from her book,
Revolution From Within
published by Little, Brown & Co.

The **Rev. Norman Vincent Peale**
passed away on Christmas Eve, 1993.
He was a minister, well-known author,
and a motivational speaker.

"I can do it if I truly think I
can."

Mary Kay Ash is the Founder and
Chairwoman Emeritus of Mary Kay Cosmetics.

A leader has two important
characteristics:
first,
she is going somewhere;
second,
she is able to persuade others
to go with her.

-unknown

William C. Westmoreland's *distinguished
military career included service to his country as
the Superintendent of the United States Military
Academy at West Point, commander of American
forces in Vietnam, and Army Chief-of-Staff.*

Do onto others
as you would have them
do unto you.

*-The Golden Rule,
based on Matthew 7:12 and found in
similar forms in ancient Jewish, Greek,
and Chinese writings*

*Olympic Gold Medalist **Mike Barrowman** set the world record while winning the 200 meter breast stroke at the 1992 Summer Olympics in Madrid, Spain.*

"You can have anything you want in this life. You must, however, be prepared to pay for it. You can go to the moon if you want it bad enough... but be prepared to spend every waking hour making the money to get there, as well as training for the event.
You could also choose a much easier goal, such as to become an Olympic champion. This would only require a small portion of your lifetime.
Then again, you may just want a hamburger -
that's only a dollar."

Many knowledgeable observers rate
Richard Lee Petty *as the greatest stock*
car driver ever.

"A winner can smile all the time, but it takes a real winner to smile when you lose."

T. Boone Pickens *is an entrepreneur extraordinare.*

"Keep driving until you hear glass breaking."

Anna Quindlen's column appears in the *New York Times and is syndicated to newspapers nationwide. She is also a bestselling author.*

In spite of everything I still believe that people are really good at heart.

-Anne Frank

Sally Jessy Raphael *is a nationally syndicated TV talk show host.*

Laugh, and the world laughs with you.
Weep, and you weep alone.
For this sad old earth must borrow its mirth,
It has troubles enough of its own.

-from the poem Solitude,
by Ella Wheeler Wilcox

Orville Redenbacher *is the popcorn entrepreneur whose product bears his name.*

"Do one thing, and do it better than anyone else."

Frank Shorter *won the gold medal in the marathon at the 1972 Summer Olympics in Munich.*

"Consistency is the key."

Dave Thomas is the Founder and Senior Chairman of the Board of Wendy's.

"*You can be whatever you want to be within the laws of God and Man* is a saying that continues to have a strong impact on my life. To me it means follow your dreams, don't give up on your goals, and you can succeed with honesty and integrity as your guiding forces. It's especially true in America where you truly can be whatever you want if you're dedicated, hardworking and honest."

Joey Reiman is the Chairman and Chief Executive Officer of the Joey Reiman Agency, an advertising agency in Atlanta. He is also an author and a motivational speaker.

"The Safe Way is a grocery store."

Fred Rogers *is the host of the children's television show "Mr. Roger's Neighborhood."*

L'essentiel est invisible pour les yeux. (Translation: What is essential is invisible to the eye.)

> *-from the book Le Petit Prince by Antoine de St. Exupery*

Interestingly, author and noted speaker
Dr. Leo F. Buscaglia *sent in the same*
quote from Le Petit Prince. Dr. Buscaglia's
response included an additional sentence.

It is only with the heart
that one sees rightly.
What is essential
is invisible to the eye.

*Investment banker **William Simon** served as Secretary of the Treasury under President Ford. Simon is also an author and popular speaker.*

In the end, more than they wanted freedom, they wanted security. They wanted a comfortable life and they lost it all - security, comfort and freedom. When the Athenians finally wanted not to give to society but for society to give to them, when the freedom they wished for most was freedom from responsibility, then Athens ceased to be free.

-Edward Gibbon, writing of ancient Greece

Dave Barry *is a syndicated columnist,*
bestselling author, and a very funny guy.

It's better to be
rich and healthy
than poor and sick.

-Dave Barry's mom

*Band leader and trumpet player **Doc Severinsen** provided several sayings that have been important in his life.*

Easy does it!

-Alcoholics Anonymous

"I have a little saying of my own that I recite every morning before my feet hit the floor: *In this entire day, I will allow nothing to upset me.*"

"A well known comic of about 20 years ago, Jackie Vernon, had a saying which was rather amusing too. He always used to conclude his performances by quoting his favorite uncle as having said: *A wet bird never flies at night.* I don't think Jackie would mind being quoted in your book."

Dr. Bernie S. Siegel's favorite saying came from his mother. Dr. Siegel is a bestselling author who has written extensively on the importance of one's attitude and faith when confronted with serious illness.

It was meant to be.
God is redirecting you.
Something good
will come of this.

                              -Rose Siegel

Hank Williams, Jr. is a musician and songwriter.

"If you want to make it,
you can't fake it.
You've got to live it!"

Sargent Shriver *was the first director of both the Peace Corps and the Office of Economic Opportunity. He served as the United States ambassador to France from 1968-1970, and was the Democratic candidate for Vice President in 1972.*

Bring me only bad news.
Good news weakens me.

> *-Charles Kettering,*
> *a founder of General Motors*

Scott Turow is an attorney and bestselling author. His books include <u>One L</u>, <u>Presumed Innocent</u>, <u>The Burden of Proof</u>, and <u>Pleading Guilty</u>.

There is no such thing as a free lunch.

> -often attributed to economist
> Milton Freidman

"Even when life is good, it isn't easy."

Bruce Williams hosts a nationally syndicated radio talk show. Williams is also an author and an entrepreneur.

"Consider the turtle.
He never gets anywhere ...
unless he sticks his neck out."

Peggy Say *was an activist on behalf of Americans held hostage in Lebanon.*

There may be times when we are powerless to prevent injustice, but there must never come a time when we fail to protest.

-Elie Wiesel

John Wooden is the only man to be elected to the Naismith Memorial Basketball Hall of Fame as both a coach and player. While coaching the U.C.L.A. Bruins, Wooden's teams won a record 10 N.C.A.A. titles including 7 straight championships from 1967-73. Wooden was a 3-time All-American guard at Purdue from 1930-32.

MAKING THE MOST OF ONE'S SELF

Be true to yourself.
Make each day your masterpiece.
Help others.
Drink deeply from good books.
Make friendship a fine art.
Build a shelter against a rainy day.
Pray for guidance and give thanks for your blessings every day.

-given to Wooden by his father when Wooden graduated from grade school

Joe Neely compiled the sayings in this book. He couldn't resist including his own favorite saying.

In the midst of winter,
I finally learned there was,
in me,
an invincible summer.

-*Albert Camus*